Summer for All

Building Coordinated Networks to Promote Access to Quality Summer Learning and Enrichment Opportunities Across a Community

Catherine H. Augustine, Jennifer Sloan McCombs, Garrett Baker

Commissioned by

For more information on this publication, visit **www.rand.org/t/RRA205-1**.

About RAND

The RAND Corporation is a research organization that develops solutions to public policy challenges to help make communities throughout the world safer and more secure, healthier and more prosperous. RAND is nonprofit, nonpartisan, and committed to the public interest. To learn more about RAND, visit www.rand.org.

Research Integrity

Our mission to help improve policy and decisionmaking through research and analysis is enabled through our core values of quality and objectivity and our unwavering commitment to the highest level of integrity and ethical behavior. To help ensure our research and analysis are rigorous, objective, and nonpartisan, we subject our research publications to a robust and exacting quality-assurance process; avoid both the appearance and reality of financial and other conflicts of interest through staff training, project screening, and a policy of mandatory disclosure; and pursue transparency in our research engagements through our commitment to the open publication of our research findings and recommendations, disclosure of the source of funding of published research, and policies to ensure intellectual independence. For more information, visit www.rand.org/about/principles.

RAND's publications do not necessarily reflect the opinions of its research clients and sponsors.

Published by the RAND Corporation, Santa Monica, Calif.
© 2021 RAND Corporation
RAND® is a registered trademark.

Library of Congress Cataloging-in-Publication Data is available for this publication.

ISBN: 978-1-9774-0811-2

Cover image credit: Jim Mendenhall/The Wallace Foundation; Back cover credit: FatCamera/Getty Images

ABOUT THIS REPORT

This study was commissioned by The Wallace Foundation, which seeks to support and share effective ideas and practices to foster equity and improvements in learning and enrichment for young people, and in the arts for everyone. The Foundation's current objectives are to improve the quality of schools, primarily by developing and placing effective principals in high-need schools; improve the quality of and access to afterschool programs through coordinated city systems and by strengthening the financial management skills of providers; reimagine and expand learning time during the traditional school day and year, as well as during the summer months; expand access to arts learning; and develop audiences for the arts. For more information and research on these and other related topics, please visit the Foundation's Knowledge Center at www.wallacefoundation.org.

The Wallace Foundation launched the National Summer Learning Project (NSLP) in 2011 to expand summer program opportunities for low-income students in urban districts and to study the effectiveness of district-led summer programs and how they could be well implemented. Through the NSLP, The Wallace Foundation has provided support to public school districts and their community partners in Boston; Dallas; Duval County, Florida; Pittsburgh; and Rochester, New York.

The Wallace Foundation engaged our RAND Corporation research team to assess the effectiveness of these districts' voluntary, district-led summer learning programs, and we found, using experimental analyses, near-term academic benefits in mathematics for all students. Using correlational analyses, we also found academic benefits in mathematics that persisted through the school year for high attenders and additional benefits after the second summer of programming in mathematics, reading, and social-emotional competencies, again for students with high attendance. The implementation data we collected allowed us to describe how to design, launch, and lead strong summer learning programs that benefit children. As part of the NSLP, we continued to track students three years after the programs ended, when students reached the end of seventh grade. We found that the magnitude of the advantage that high attenders held over comparable students in the control group had decreased and was no

The Wallace Foundation launched the National Summer Learning Project (NSLP) in 2011 to expand summer program opportunities for low-income students in urban districts.

longer statistically significant; however, the magnitude of the advantage of high attendance remained educationally meaningful (McCombs et al., 2020).

In 2019, the National Academies of Sciences, Engineering, and Medicine released a consensus study report regarding summer experiences and how they shape the development and well-being of children and youth (National Academies of Sciences, Engineering, and Medicine, 2019a). One of the key recommendations in the report is for cities and counties to take a comprehensive, communitywide approach to ensuring that the needs of their children and youth are adequately met during the summer. As the NSLP wound down, some of the districts turned their attention and efforts toward sustaining their progress in promoting program scale and quality. To further sustainability, some of these districts and their partners are part of regional networks working to expand opportunities for quality summer programming in their cities. In this report, we chronicle the early efforts of these districts and their partners toward creating coordinated approaches to increasing access to quality summer learning, noting their challenges, enablers, and early outcomes. We aim to help city and county leaders, district leaders, and out-of-school time intermediaries launch and sustain such coordinated networks.

We aim to help city and county leaders, district leaders, and out-of-school time intermediaries launch and sustain such coordinated networks.

This report is the eighth in RAND's Summer Learning Series. The first report, *Getting to Work on Summer Learning: Recommended Practices for Success* (Augustine et al., 2013) offered lessons learned from detailed, formative evaluations of the NSLP district programs in summer 2011. These evaluations, shared originally with districts in fall 2011, were designed to help summer leaders improve the programs that they offered in 2012. We completed another set of evaluations of the 2012 summer programs so that the districts could further strengthen their programs by summer 2013, when we launched a randomized controlled trial to assess program effects on students' school-year performances. The second report, *Ready for Fall? Near-Term Effects of Voluntary Summer Learning Programs on Low-Income Students' Learning Opportunities and Outcomes* (McCombs et al., 2014), looked at how NSLP students performed on mathematics, reading, and social-emotional assessments in fall 2013, after one summer of programming. The third report, *Learning from Summer: Effects of Voluntary Summer Learning Programs on Low-Income Urban*

Youth (Augustine et al., 2016), examined student outcomes at four different times: fall 2013, at the end of the 2013–2014 school year, fall 2014 after the second summer of programming, and at the end of the 2014–2015 school year. The fourth report, *Making Summer Last: Integrating Summer Programming into Core District Priorities and Operations* (Augustine and Thompson, 2017), examined how summer program leaders are integrating their programs into their districts' core priorities and operations as a sustainability strategy. The fifth report, the second edition of *Getting to Work on Summer Learning* (Schwartz et al., 2018), updated our first report based on implementation and outcomes analyses of the NSLP programs in summers 2013 and 2014. The sixth report, *Getting Support for Summer Learning* (Augustine and Thompson, 2020), examined policies at the federal, state, and local levels that support or constrain the ability of districts to scale and sustain summer programs. The seventh report, *Every Summer Counts* (McCombs et al., 2020), presented a longitudinal follow-up of the NSLP student outcomes three school years after the end of the second summer of programming.

RAND Education and Labor

This research was undertaken by RAND Education and Labor, a division of the RAND Corporation that conducts research on early childhood through postsecondary education programs, workforce development, and programs and policies affecting workers, entrepreneurship, and financial literacy and decisionmaking.

More information about RAND can be found at www.rand.org. Questions about this report should be directed to Catherine Augustine (catherine_augustine@rand.org) and questions about RAND Education and Labor should be directed to educationandlabor@rand.org.

Acknowledgments

We would like to thank Ann Stone, Lucas Held, and Dan Browne at The Wallace Foundation for their valuable guidance on this work and for other substantive and financial support.

We thank our RAND colleagues who contributed to this report. Stephanie Lonsinger assisted with editing. During the quality assurance and production process, Fatih Unlu and Andrea P. Tuma provided a careful review and valuable feedback. Arwen Bicknell edited the final document, Kristen Meadows formatted the document and cover, and Monette Velasco shepherded the report through production.

Our external peer reviewer, Deborah Moroney, also provided excellent feedback.

Finally, we thank the network leaders in Boston, Massachusetts; Dallas, Texas; Pittsburgh, Pennsylvania; and Washington, D.C., for their participation in the study and dedication to the children in their communities.

Contents

SUMMARY

Summer is a time of opportunity and risk for children and youth. Today and in years past, children whose families are experiencing poverty have fewer opportunities for academic, cultural, athletic, and other activities than do their more affluent peers, and these children are more likely to face food insecurity and reside in unsafe neighborhoods. In 2021, there is an even greater emphasis on summer programming as policymakers and practitioners turn their energy toward accelerating learning and development as we emerge from the global coronavirus pandemic. The American Rescue Plan provides funding for summer learning (U.S. Department of Education, undated), recognizing the opportunity that this time frame presents. Over the next three years, states and school districts can spend approximately $30 billion more on out-of-school time (OST) programming than they have in the past from the extra aid for students in kindergarten through 12th grade provided in the stimulus measure signed in March 2021.

Funding is available for both schools and for local community organizations. Community partners can augment academic summer programs with interest- and skill-building opportunities that are not typically available to children and youth experiencing poverty. In addition, community partners offer their own summer programs that can expand access to opportunities more generally. The National Academies of Sciences, Engineering, and Medicine (2019b, p. 1) has recommended that cities coordinate their summer efforts among multiple community organizations to expand citywide access to quality summer programming.

The purpose of this report is to explain how organizations in four cities were doing exactly that—coordinating their efforts to collectively increase access to quality summer programs—and to inform leaders in cities throughout the country.

The seeds for this study were planted in 2010, when The Wallace Foundation first began to address the inequity in access to summer opportunities for young people. The Foundation initiated the National Summer Learning Project (NSLP) in Boston; Dallas; Duval County, Florida; Pittsburgh; and Rochester, New York, to expand such opportunities for students whose families were experiencing poverty and to understand whether and how summer

The seeds for this study were planted in 2010, when The Wallace Foundation first began to address the inequity in access to summer opportunities for young people.

programs can improve outcomes for participants. We assessed the effectiveness of these voluntary, district-led summer learning programs, and we found not only that attendees benefited in terms of both their academic and social-emotional outcomes but also what it takes to run effective programs.

As the NSLP wound down, some of the school districts and their community partners accelerated their work with other city leaders to attract more students in their communities into a diverse array of quality summer programs. In these cities, several leaders—such as mayors; city council members; and school district, OST intermediary, library, and community-based organization heads—recognized the general need to create, strengthen, and promote summer programming for children and youth. In some cities, these groups identified specific populations or neighborhoods with the greatest need.

Such coordination brings a more diverse set of resources to bear on a given problem, capitalizing on the skills and competencies represented by different types of organizations. We use the term *coordinated networks* to describe a constellation of individuals, agencies, and organizations that are led by one or more of the member organizations in working together to accomplish a shared goal—in this case, greater access to quality summer programs.

In 2017, we interviewed representatives from three of the NSLP cities (Boston, Dallas, and Pittsburgh) that were undertaking this citywide work. We also investigated similar citywide efforts in Washington, D.C. These interviews form the basis of this report.

Our goal was to identify the ways that organizations in the four cities collaborated, their goals, how they went about achieving those goals, and what successes and roadblocks came up along the way. The following research questions guided our exploration:

- How have cities developed collaborative efforts to strengthen and promote summer opportunities?

- What progress have these efforts made?

- What challenges have these networks faced?

- What lessons have emerged from this work that might benefit other cities?

Our goal was to identify the ways that organizations in the four cities collaborated, their goals, how they went about achieving those goals, and what successes and roadblocks came up along the way.

We synthesized other studies of coordinated networks to distill common indicators or enablers of success. Using this review, we set out to determine how the coordinated networks in the cities we were studying **developed** a **shared vision** and **strong leadership, coordinated** their **work, raised funds to sustain the work,** and **collected** and analyzed **diagnostic data** to gauge their progress.

In each of the cities we studied, the organizations working together had at least some prior experience coordinating with one another to elevate the importance of summer services for youth and communities. As a result, galvanizing a more coordinated effort around summer was a relatively easy next step, particularly with mayoral support. Mayors in these cities served as strong, visible leaders of this work. They engaged media, influenced funders, and commanded the respect and diligence of multiple organizations and individuals. Individuals from partner organizations in these cities—school districts, city agencies, libraries, advocacy organizations, organizations that served as coordinating intermediaries, and others—provided skilled leadership, strengthening existing networks and drawing in new partners.

The goals of the coordinated efforts varied and focused on such things as raising awareness about summer programming in the community, improving program quality, and increasing access to and participation in summer programs. Neighborhood safety and community engagement were also goals in some cases.

The networks we studied organized into one of three different types of structures: intragovernmental department coordination, intermediary-led coordination, and multi-organization collaborative. All these structures demonstrated success. However, the two intermediary-led networks were farther along in their quality improvement efforts, perhaps because of their fundraising success.

Through their efforts, the networks raised awareness of summer opportunities throughout their cities and provided information to families about specific programs. The number of children and youth participating in summer programming in these cities increased, and new programs were developed in high-need areas. There were also signs that more attention was being paid to summer opportunities by funders and policymakers. Network leaders made impressive strides in continuous improvement models and supported individual programs' quality development.

All these collaborative efforts remained strong through summer 2019 and have, to our knowledge, continued supporting providers as they pivoted to virtual program options during the coronavirus pandemic.

Even with these successes, establishing and maintaining buy-in for collaborative work requires ongoing effort. Leadership and fundraising models were sometimes questioned by individual program providers who saw themselves as competing against the networks for local foundation funding. Sustainability was also a challenge, causing some networks to rethink their approaches to quality improvement efforts, which can be costly. It took effort to keep partners informed and moving in the same direction. Despite such challenges, the networks have continued to do this work for several more years—an indication of the durability of such efforts.

The cities' experiences suggest that citywide coordination among youth-focused organizations could help increase awareness of, attention to, participation in, and improvements to summer learning programs.

Recommendations

This report provides recommendations that are based on how the studied communities worked to increase access to quality summer programs. We target organizational leaders in other cities who want to develop or strengthen coordinated networks. Our recommendations focus on launching a coordinated network, setting and achieving goals, promoting equity, and gathering and using data to assess progress. These recommendations are targeted to those wanting to increase participation in quality summer opportunities but might be relevant to other types of networks as well.

Launching a Coordinated Network

Set a broad vision that allows for strategic evolution. The vision for summer programming remained consistent in each of the cities; however, strategies for achieving these visions shifted. As some networks matured, they spent less time on improving access to programming and more time on the quality of programming. Others moved away from specific activities, such as competency-based badging, without abandoning the vision of increasing participation in quality summer opportunities. We recommend adopting this flexibility as a network matures and its members learn more about the needs of its particular locale.

Garner mayoral support for the citywide effort. One strategy used by all network leaders was involving the city's mayor. Mayors set communitywide goals for student participation in summer programs, asked to be kept apprised of progress, made summer programming a mayoral initiative, assigned staff to take on such tasks as creating and hosting program locators on city websites, and made public statements about the importance of summer programming.

Leverage the experiences of past local coordination efforts. The efforts we studied were built on established relationships. In general, we recommend reflecting on the established relationships in a given place and modeling new networks on those that have worked in the past, expanding these relationships to invite new people and organizations connected to summer programming.

Setting and Achieving Goals

Align the goals and strategies to the organizational structure of the coordinated effort. We found that different organizational structures—such as intragovernmental department coordination, intermediary-led coordination, and multi-organization collaboratives—can be effective. In some cases, the cities capitalized on a given structure to accomplish goals that could only be supported by that particular structure. For instance, in Washington, D.C., which established intragovernmental department coordination, the city was able to target residents of all ages and use strategies that required city government leverage because the mayor asked the leaders of schools, human services, the police department, and parks and recreation to meet every other week from January through the summer to set goals and report on progress. It would have taken much more effort in the other cities to involve these other departments—it might have been possible, but the structure in the District of Columbia made it feasible.

Align strategies to goals for summer programming. In addition to considering how the structure of a citywide effort supports goals and strategies, the goals and strategies themselves should align. For example, if a citywide goal is to promote greater access

In general, we recommend reflecting on the established relationships in a given place and modeling new networks on those that have worked in the past, expanding these relationships to invite new people and organizations connected to summer programming.

to quality summer programming opportunities, there should be coordinated city work aimed at determining and/or increasing the number of participants *and* improving the quality of programming. Furthermore, if the goal is to increase access for populations that have not historically had it, communities need to measure progress by neighborhood, income level, or another demographic of interest rather than overall increases in participation. If improving quality is an important goal, there should be a way to measure improvements.

Carefully consider strategies and the resources needed to implement them well. Each strategy adopted requires a set of conditions that are necessary to ensure robust implementation. For instance, adopting a program locator requires (1) technological expertise, (2) the ability to populate the database with program information each year, (3) sufficient community awareness to make it a valued resource, and (4) sufficient resources to invest in development, incentives for providers, and marketing. Without meeting these conditions, implementation could fail and might not be worth the investment of time and resources.

Promoting Equity

Consider targeting efforts to neighborhoods with the greatest need. Two of the cities we studied focused their efforts on specific neighborhoods, and interviewees there described being able to develop partnerships and programs in areas with the most need (e.g., those with high poverty or crime rates). Focusing on neighborhoods where residents and youth are facing the most-adverse circumstances might address the most-pressing needs in a more comprehensive manner than could be accomplished if tackling an entire city at once. Developing more programs in areas of high need also might reduce the necessity of finding low-cost, reliable transportation for children and youth to leave these neighborhoods for program opportunities.

Developing more programs in areas of high need also might reduce the necessity of finding low-cost, reliable transportation for children and youth to leave these neighborhoods for program opportunities.

Gathering and Using Data to Assess Progress

Determine how to assess progress early in the process. We recommend developing an evaluation plan early, specifying the data needed to assess achievement of goals and then ensuring that staffing and data structures are in place to support the plan. If, for example, a goal is to improve access to quality programs, leaders of citywide efforts should start by developing mechanisms for defining quality and continually assessing and improving programs. Three of the cities we focused on strove to improve quality, and each made impressive strides toward this goal. In the cities with the most-advanced work on quality improvement, network leaders had raised significant new funding. These dollars supported such activities as observing program instruction, surveying teachers about students' social-emotional learning competencies, providing tailored evaluation reports to individual programs, and hosting professional development sessions.

Create incentives to ensure summer program provider buy-in. Citywide efforts often require program provider buy-in. Program leaders might be called on to deliver data, expand programs, and participate in quality-improvement efforts. We recommend adopting the strategies that our interviewees found successful in incentivizing individual program providers to join the networks, such as offering
(1) funding, (2) participation and outcome data reports to individual providers for their own use, (3) professional development and networking activities, and (4) videos or high-resolution photographs of program activities that could be used in subsequent marketing efforts. Achieving program provider buy-in helps network leaders measure progress toward meeting their goals and could also help in improving program quality.

CHAPTER ONE

Introduction

S ummer is a time of opportunity and risk for children and youth; however, the opportunities and risks are not spread proportionately across the population. During the summer, children whose families are experiencing poverty have fewer opportunities for academic, cultural, athletic, and other activities than do their more affluent peers, and these children are also more likely to face food insecurity and spend time in unsafe neighborhoods. A 2019 National Academies of Sciences, Engineering, and Medicine report highlights the critical nature of summer experiences to the academic, health, safety, and social-emotional outcomes for children; the critical need for summer services for children living in less-advantageous circumstances; and the potential for various agents across the community to innovate and coordinate to better serve these children (National Academies of Sciences, Engineering, and Medicine, 2019a).

In response to the inequity in access to summer opportunities for young people, The Wallace Foundation initiated the National Summer Learning Project (NSLP) in 2010 to expand such opportunities for students whose families were experiencing poverty and to determine whether and how summer programs can improve outcomes for participants. In spring 2011, the Foundation selected and began funding school districts and their community partners in five cities: Boston; Dallas; Duval County, Florida; Pittsburgh; and Rochester, New York.

> We found, using experimental analyses, near-term statistically significant academic benefits in mathematics for all students.

The Wallace Foundation engaged the RAND Corporation to assess the effectiveness of these voluntary, district-led summer learning programs. We found, using experimental analyses, near-term statistically significant academic benefits in mathematics for all students. We also found that statistically significant academic benefits in mathematics persisted through the school year after the first summer for students with high attendance. After the second summer of programming, we found statistically significant benefits in mathematics, reading, and social-emotional competencies for high attenders. Because of the implementation data we had collected, we were able to determine the key components of successful summer learning programs. As part of the NSLP, we tracked students' performance from third grade through two summers of programming to three school years after the program ended, when they reached the end of seventh grade. We found that the magnitude of the advantage high attenders held over comparable students in the control group had decreased and was no longer statistically significant but remained educationally meaningful (McCombs et al., 2020).

Although the district programs serve thousands of students, attendees make up just a fraction of youth who reside in these communities. As the NSLP wound down, some of the districts and their community partners worked with other city leaders to turn their attention and efforts toward ensuring that more students in their communities could benefit from quality summer programming.

In these cities, several leaders—such as mayors; city council members; and school district, out-of-school time (OST) intermediary, library, and community-based organization (CBO) heads—recognized the general need to create, strengthen, and promote summer programming for children and youth from low-income families. They also identified specific neighborhoods with greater needs. They attempted to collectively recruit more youth into quality summer programs to address such needs, notably academic, social-emotional, physical health, and safety needs.

In 2017, we interviewed representatives from three of the NSLP cities (Boston, Dallas, and Pittsburgh) who were undertaking this citywide work. In addition to studying these three cities, we investigated similar citywide efforts in Washington, D.C., as a way to incorporate a government agency–led model in our research. These interviews form the basis of this report.

Coordinated networks arise when individual organizations realize that they cannot enact large-scale change on their own. In many cities across the country, organizations have coordinated to address social problems in their local contexts. Coordinated action is sometimes a response to a problem that has risen to the top of multiple organizations' priority lists. Henig et al. lists "perception of crisis" as one of three preconditions for cross-sector collaboration, describing it as the "[w]idespread sense that the problem has reached a point at which a new approach is necessary" (Henig et al., 2016, p. 7). This sense of a pressing and complex need in a community can spur coordination across organizations.

Such coordination brings a more diverse set of resources to bear on the problem, capitalizing on the skills and competencies represented by different types of organizations. Bodilly and Augustine assert that "[a]ny organization that sets a goal of serving all children [in a given region] must involve different types of organizations in planning to achieve that goal" (Bodilly and Augustine, 2008, p. 63). Coordinated networks vary in the depth and breadth of membership from place to place, and many types of organizations could be involved. In the case of summer programming, for example, city governments could garner awareness and address policy questions; school districts could ensure a focus on academics; and nonprofits could identify partners focused on skill building and other nonacademic enrichment programming as well as raise funds and launch quality improvement campaigns.

We use the term *coordinated networks* to describe a constellation of individuals, agencies, and organizations, led by one or more of the member organizations, working together to accomplish a shared goal.

Frameworks for Coordinated Networks and Systems

Prior research suggests several factors that enable coordinated community efforts. Here, we describe some of that research and the resulting commonalities among their findings and frameworks. Common indicators of success that emerge across several studies of coordinated networks are **shared vision**, **strong leadership**, **coordinated action**, **funding for sustainability**, and collecting **diagnostic data**.

For example, in a study of early OST systems-building in five communities (Bodily et al., 2010), researchers found that coordinated systems that led to improved access and quality were characterized by

- a common vision among stakeholders

- an early assessment of needs

- a system to manage and track data

- active support of the mayor

- buy-in from stakeholders (particularly schools)

- funding.

Similar findings emerge from a review of multiple networks. Kania and Kramer (2011) describe five key elements of coordinated networks:

1. a **common agenda** for change, with a shared understanding of the problem and a joint approach to solving it through agreed-on actions

2. data collection and **consistent measurement of results** across all the participants to ensure alignment and accountability

3. a plan of action that outlines and coordinates **mutually reinforcing activities** for each participant

4. open and **continuous communication** across the many players to build trust, ensure mutual objectives, and create common motivation

5. a **backbone organization(s)** with staff and a specific set of skills to serve the entire initiative and coordinate participating organizations and agencies.

The authors also note that funders often focus on near-term change and that coordinated networks must have funders dedicated to the long term to "help create and sustain the collective processes, measurement reporting systems, and community leadership that enable cross-sector coalitions to arise and thrive" (Kania and Kramer, 2011, p. 41).

The National Summer Learning Association (NSLA) specifies six indicators of successful efforts to build citywide systems of summer learning opportunities:

1. a shared vision and citywide coordination

2. engaged leadership

3. a data management system

4. continuous quality improvement

5. sustainable resources

6. marketing and communications (NSLA, 2016).

Regarding sustainability, NSLA outlines the important role that funding plays, and it specifically recommends that the coordinated network be supported by at least four of the following sources: local private foundations, business donations and sponsorships, local public funding, national foundations, state funding, and federal funding (NSLA, 2016).

Although all the frameworks note the need for data, measuring certain outcomes is difficult. Youth outcomes, such as improved social skills or academic learning, can be challenging to measure across an entire city and are often affected by conditions outside the program. Even if it is possible to measure a particular outcome, it is difficult to determine a causal link between that outcome and the program because of a lack of data on comparable nonparticipants. Henig et al. (2016) reported on eight early-phase collaborations and arrived at this same conclusion. Not surprisingly, many initiatives that are focused on children and youth opt to measure process and participation outcomes rather than final youth outcomes.

As another example, the Campaign for Grade-Level Reading (CGLR) issued a report (2017) in which it found that, reading proficiency had increased among low-income children since the campaign began in 2010,[1] although the reading proficiency gap between high- and low-income students remained. However, it is difficult to determine whether CGLR directly influenced this

> Youth outcomes, such as improved social skills or academic learning, can be challenging to measure across an entire city and are often affected by conditions outside the program.

---

[1] Between 2009, the year before CGLR began, and 2015, low-income students gained in reading proficiency on the National Assessment of Educational Progress, also known as The Nation's Report Card (CGLR, 2017). The proportion of low-income fourth-graders who met the proficiency standard increased from 17 percent to 21 percent in reading.

increase in the reading proficiency rate. According to CGLR leaders, there had been an increase in the number of volunteers providing tutoring in reading, school superintendents signing pledges to improve grade-level reading proficiency, CGLR newsletter subscriptions and downloads, and policymakers highlighting reading as an important issue. CGLR suggests that these activities have led to more students reading at grade level by third grade and expects they will continue to do so, but this is incredibly challenging to prove.

If a network sets a goal of increasing access to quality summer program opportunities for those who have historically lacked it, then it might be most feasible to measure the number of participants and improvements in individual program quality. Trying to measure impact in terms of social-emotional or academic outcomes is complex, time-consuming, and expensive, and efforts to do so could detract from other important community activities.

National Support for Local Coordinated Networks

As communities across the country have engaged in these types of coordinated efforts, national organizations that coordinate and provide support for these coordinated networks have emerged, such as the following:

- **Every Hour Counts**, a network of afterschool intermediaries dedicated to creating equitable, expanded access to quality expanded learning programs. It provides its community members with a set of resources, including a framework for measuring the impact of their work at the system, program, and youth levels.

- **CGLR**, already introduced, is another example. It serves as an umbrella network for hundreds of community grade-level reading networks that address both in-school and out-of-school factors that prevent a significant percentage of low-income children from being at or above grade level in reading at the end of third grade. Among the network members are schools, philanthropic foundations, policymakers, government agencies, business leaders, community organizations, and other nonprofits. Summer programming is among the recommended strategies of this network.

> If a network sets a goal of increasing access to quality summer program opportunities for those who have historically lacked it, then it might be most feasible to measure the number of participants and improvements in individual program quality.

- **StriveTogether**, a nonprofit association that supports more than 70 community partnerships across the country. StriveTogether focuses on achieving racial equity and economic mobility. Its "four pillars" are (1) a shared community vision; (2) evidence-based decisionmaking; (3) collaborative action; and (4) investing in sustainability, for example by allocating people, knowledge, money, and the like to programs and services that improve outcomes and eliminate disparities (StriveTogether, 2019).

Purpose of This Report

This exploratory study investigates the early stages of coordinated networks established to strengthen and promote citywide summer program opportunities. The four cities we selected only serve as examples of how this could work; they might not be representative of networks around the country. Although we focus on the early phases of these coordinated efforts (i.e., up until summer 2016) in Boston, Dallas, Pittsburgh, and Washington, D.C., members of these networks had been addressing summer programming in various ways for several years.

The following research questions guided our exploration:

1. How have cities developed collaborative efforts to strengthen and promote summer opportunities?

2. What progress have these efforts made?

3. What challenges have these networks faced?

4. What lessons have emerged from this work that might benefit other cities?

Boston, Dallas, and Pittsburgh had participated in the NSLP, which brought citywide attention to the topic of summer learning. This might have made it easier for these cities to establish a common vision for how to continue and extend their efforts to provide quality academic summer programming. Networking efforts in Washington, D.C., were driven by the mayor, allowing for fairly smooth vision-setting and launch processes even without having participated in the NSLP. The work in each of these cities has progressed since we studied them, and we offer some snapshots of ongoing work.

We hope that this report will provide guidance to community leaders, notably government agencies, CBOs, school districts, and others working on citywide efforts to increase participation in quality summer learning opportunities in their own communities.

Approach, Data, and Methods

To address our research questions, we relied on websites, reports, documents, and data from interviews with city stakeholders. From January through March 2017, we conducted 49 interviews of 55 network participants, such as school district employees, nonprofit leaders, city government employees, and other staff from philanthropic and research organizations in our four study cities. Many interviewees managed organizations or agencies that led the coordinated networks, some were secondary participants in the networks, and others led individual summer programs. We made sure to interview the most-involved person from each organization that played a leadership role in each city's coordinated network.

We used a semistructured interview protocol. We asked individual interviewees about their own organization's work and their role in the network, the origin and evolution of the network, the network goals, the planning process, network leadership and participation, outreach to families and youth, programming, costs, perceived impacts of the network, factors that facilitated success, challenges, and recommendations for other cities.

Interviews lasted between 20 minutes and one hour depending on the interviewee's depth of knowledge. We conducted most of our interviews in person during scheduled site visits, but some interviews were conducted over the phone. By interviewee consent, we audio recorded and took notes during all interviews, relying on the recordings to fill gaps in our notes.

We analyzed our interview notes using Dedoose v7.5.26, a web-based application for mixed-methods research. The first round of coding was based on the interview questions. Additional themes emerged from the interviews, and we conducted a second round of coding based on these themes. The final code list featured such topics as actions of the initiative, challenges, costs, data collected, and facilitators of success. Using the coding results, we developed city-level cases, examining agreement and disagreement among interviewees. We then conducted a cross-case analysis to find themes that emerged across cities.

Our goal was to identify the ways that organizations in these four cities collaborated, what their goals were, how they went about achieving those goals, and what successes and roadblocks came up along the way. Our intent was not to create another framework to guide collaboration but to provide current and nuanced examples of goals, the actions taken to meet them, challenges, and successes. We aim to provide useful information to other organizations that hope to pursue a similar endeavor in their community.

Although we hope that the examples and recommendations of this exploratory study will be broadly useful, we recognize their limitations. We only studied four cities, and three were selected based on convenience (they were part of the larger NSLP initiative). These three, plus Washington, D.C., were described by national experts, however, as having some of the most sophisticated citywide systems promoting summer learning opportunities. This made them worthy of study but perhaps not generalizable. Our findings might be most applicable to other midsized, urban cities. Furthermore, we only interviewed 55 people; their views might not be representative of other views held in these cities. Finally, we conducted these interviews in 2017, before the onset of the coronavirus pandemic. Although we have collected information about these cities' ongoing efforts, we know less about how they considered and promoted summer learning programs in recent years.

We do not intend for this report to represent all the ways in which organizations can collaborate on expanding access to quality summer programming. Nor do we intend for this report to be treated as an evaluation of these networks and the summer programs they provide.

In the next section, we introduce the four cities' coordinated networks, followed by a more detailed description of each. We then use our synthesis of the aforementioned frameworks to investigate the progress and challenges in each city. We end with our conclusions and recommendations based on study findings to help inform other city leaders who might be considering similar coordinated efforts in their communities.

Our goal was to identify the ways that organizations in these four cities collaborated, what their goals were, how they went about achieving those goals, and what successes and roadblocks came up along the way.

CHAPTER TWO

The Four Networks

I n this chapter, we describe the four citywide initiatives. We explain the evolution of each coordinated network; introduce its key stakeholders and participants; describe its goals, marketing efforts, and other activities leading up to summer 2016; and discuss perceived impacts. Each of these initiatives has continued to evolve since 2016; we conclude each city-specific discussion with a text box to provide relevant updates.

Boston Summer Learning Community

Boston began a coordinated citywide effort to increase access to quality summer programing in 2010. Its focus on summer opportunities emerged following an effort to create a communitywide vision for the skills that youth need to succeed in school, college, and careers; these skills included critical thinking, self-regulation, and perseverance (Boston After School & Beyond, undated).

Boston After School & Beyond is an OST intermediary that coordinates with partners and OST programs to improve access to quality OST programming throughout the city in collaboration with the United Way, the City of Boston, and Boston Public Schools (BPS). This intermediary engaged the community to develop a summer programming vision, which resulted in the Achieve-Connect-Thrive (ACT) Skills Framework being established in 2008.

In 2008, a small group of community leaders from Boston After School & Beyond, BPS, the Barr Foundation, and leaders of the Boston Opportunity Agenda (a local public-private partnership working to transform the Boston education landscape from cradle to career) began meeting every week to discuss the ACT Skills Framework. The conversations began to focus on summer because of concerns that this period increased opportunity and achievement gaps between youth from low-income families and youth from higher-income families. Summer was also seen as an opportune time for innovation and partnership. As one interviewee noted:

> [Summer is] a place where schools and community-based organizations can own the space in a more equal way; it's nobody's turf or territory.

These weekly meetings became more formalized over time as the group began to plan a concrete pilot for summer programming that operated in partnership with schools and CBOs, focused on supporting social-emotional learning (SEL) and academic learning.

In summer 2010, Boston After School & Beyond and BPS launched a summer learning program, using funding from the Boston Opportunity Agenda, that served 232 students from five schools. The program goal was to increase access to and participation in high-quality summer programs in the city. In 2011, Boston After School & Beyond and BPS received funding from The Wallace Foundation as part of the NSLP to expand and strengthen summer programming.

In 2013, Boston After School & Beyond launched what it referred to as a "quality network" of summer program providers that shared a set of quality and student outcome measures and engaged in continuous program improvement. By creating a network around shared goals for program quality and youth outcomes, Boston After School & Beyond was able to attract summer providers into the network even if they did not receive funding through Boston After School & Beyond (which served as a pass-through organization for some of the funding going to summer programming). Over time, the number of programs in the quality network has expanded, and fewer receive funding through Boston After School & Beyond. By 2019, the network featured 160 sites that served 14,000 students.

In summer 2010, Boston After School & Beyond and BPS launched a summer learning program, using funding from the Boston Opportunity Agenda, that served 232 students from five schools.

City Partners and Their Roles

The Boston Summer Learning Community involves several partners across the city:

- Boston After School & Beyond serves as the coordinating entity and provides the staff that leads the continuous improvement and outreach efforts.

- BPS is a lead partner and works to give CBOs access to school staff and students. The district directly oversees all district-funded summer programs, all of which provide full-day programming that features academic instruction and enrichment activities run in collaboration with CBOs.

- The local funding community, which consists of local foundations and businesses, provides funding for specific summer programs and, in the early years, supported research efforts.

- City leaders, including the mayor and the mayor's cabinet members, provide high-level input and broadly promote the importance of summer for children and youth.

- CBOs operate the summer programs, conduct continuous improvement, and helped to launch the early programs that developed into the network.

Goals and Related Activities

Boston's collaborative work was built on the goals of (1) expanding access to and participation in high-quality summer learning opportunities and (2) creating a shared commitment to collaborative learning. Network members share a common definition of program quality, and they measure student participation, program quality, and student outcomes in alignment with Boston's ACT Skills Framework.

Participation in the network allowed programs to access student attendance tracking tools and measurement and analytic support for program quality and youth outcomes, including a program observation rubric, instructor survey, and youth survey. At the end of each summer, Boston After School & Beyond staff provided member programs with data about their program quality, child and youth attendance, and SEL outcomes in comparison with citywide benchmarks and averages. Boston After School & Beyond

Boston's collaborative work was built on the goals of (1) expanding access to and participation in high-quality summer learning opportunities and (2) creating a shared commitment to collaborative learning.

also provided targeted professional development (PD) on how to develop specific youth skills and how to use data for program improvement, and it curated and shared best practices through network sessions and an online Insight Center.

Interviewees estimated that the cost of supporting quality efforts—including maintaining databases, contracting with research partners, analyzing data, and providing PD—was approximately $375,000, or $3,000 per program. This cost was borne primarily by Boston After School & Beyond's local funders. As membership in the quality network increased and some private funding declined, supporting these costs became more challenging. Boston After School & Beyond implemented various cost-reduction strategies, such as certifying program providers to observe other programs in the network instead of having a research partner conduct those observations.

Types of Programs

All summer programs in the network were designed to develop student skills outlined in Boston's ACT Skills Framework:

- achieve goals (e.g., critical thinking, creativity, perseverance)

- connect with others (e.g., social awareness, communication, teamwork)

- thrive (e.g., growth mindset, self-efficacy, self-regulation).

The subject-matter content of the programs varied and included enrichment activities, such as sailing, robotics, reading, and outdoor activities. CBOs ran some programs in collaboration with BPS. These programs operated on a full-day, five-day-a-week schedule for five weeks; provided three hours of academic instruction daily by certified teachers; and included a set of enrichment activities in the afternoon. For example, Hale Reservation, which is a 1,137-acre nature preserve outside Boston, operated a five-week program in collaboration with BPS that included reading and mathematics instruction and camp activities, such as archery, swimming, and nature walks. In 2016, BPS expanded this model of full-day programs, offering academic instruction and enrichment activities at all its summer programs, replacing its old model of summer school.

Outcomes

A key outcome of the coordinated network was the growth in the number of students accessing high-quality summer programs and the growth of the network itself. In 2013, the Boston After School & Beyond quality network encompassed 43 summer program sites serving 2,402 students; by 2014, the network had grown to 58 sites serving 3,504 students. Between the summers of 2014 and 2015, Boston's mayor had set a goal of attracting 10,000 youth into a summer program by summer 2017. Multiple interviewees noted the benefit of the mayor's statement; one interviewee said, "When you can get the mayor committed to something in a public way, people run to it." The mayor's goal was surpassed a year early, in summer 2016, when 10,084 students in kindergarten through 12th grade participated in over 125 summer programs (Boston After School & Beyond, 2020). Although the network strove to create greater equity by expanding access for youth from low-income families, the demographics of youth served by programs across the entire network was not tracked or reported.

Interviewees discussed the myriad ways that the summer learning landscape in Boston had been affected by this coordinated network. First and foremost, interviewees reported that youth were benefiting. One interviewee described how the summer data pointed to tangible improvements in youth development:

> I know [kids] benefit in English, math, and SEL skills. They have improved relationships—they tell us, because we ask them—they have improved perseverance, improved critical thinking . . . [The programs are] helping them develop . . . socially, academically, and emotionally. We think kids get enjoyment out of it and improve their skills as a result of this. Anecdotally, we know that kids are overcoming some personal challenges through the programs, creating new connections, and increasing their social capital.

Interviewees also noted that programs were improving as a result of network participation. According to one individual,

> A key outcome of the coordinated network was the growth in the number of students accessing high-quality summer programs and the growth of the network itself.

programs are improving—kids should be getting more benefits because programs are more deliberately focusing what they do with kids, informed by what kids are saying through surveys and assessments, what observers note in the programs, and through their own appetite to get better. I think this approach has yielded more and better [programs] for kids than would otherwise be available.

Furthermore, interviewees expressed a shared sentiment that more attention was being paid to summer by funders and policymakers because of Boston After School & Beyond's quality network. For example, one interviewee relayed that a funder had denied a request for a program's funding but reversed this decision once the funder learned that the program provider was part of the quality network. Interviewees also discussed how RAND's research, which included outcomes from summer programs co-led by Boston After School & Beyond, sparked conversations in the state legislature around grant opportunities for school districts to provide summer programs.

UPDATE ON BOSTON SUMMER LEARNING COMMUNITY

The reach of the Boston After School & Beyond–led network continued to expand, serving 13,464 students across 160 programs in summer 2019, including BPS programs and programs operated by CBOs. In addition to continuing the quality and measurement work, Boston After School & Beyond also advocated for state legislation and funding for summer learning that resulted in the Massachusetts legislature and Governor Charlie Baker funding a statewide expansion of Boston's model with a $500,000 grant program in the state budget. (Boston After School & Beyond, 2020)

Dallas City of Learning

Dallas interviewees described a sizable income-based gap in youth access to summer programs and other opportunities. One interviewee described the gravity of Dallas's income gap and the work underway to identify underserved neighborhoods, including an antipoverty task force established by the mayor:

Through our partners, school district, city, and other initiatives and networks going on, we know a lot about where there is a lack of resources. There's been a lot of work done; there's been an antipoverty task force for the last couple of years. I think [there is] a . . . gap between Dallas's upper-income level and lower-income families, and that gap is widening and . . . specific zip codes in the city that are identified as the highest-density poverty areas lack all types of resources, not just summer learning and enrichment programming but health services, [healthy] food, those [kinds of] things.

Interviewees cited concerns about insufficient program opportunities in these low-income neighborhoods and raising low-income families' awareness about opportunities that did exist.

Dallas is a sprawling region and incredibly hot during the summer, which create challenges to accessing activities. One interviewee stressed that, "transportation and geography are the biggest challenges, hands down." This same interviewee compared the intense heat in Dallas with the extreme cold of "a Minnesota winter." Because of this, there are few opportunities for outdoor activities in the summer, which further challenges program providers by increasing the need for structured, indoor activities to engage youth.

Partners and Their Roles

City, school district, private local philanthropy, and nonprofit summer coordination started in Dallas in 2008 under the Thriving Minds initiative. Big Thought, a citywide intermediary organization that also provides direct programming, led this effort. Over the next few years, Big Thought and the Dallas Independent School District (DISD) developed a strong partnership to blend summer academic programming with offerings in the arts.

In 2014, Dallas stakeholders traveled to Chicago to observe how program providers there were issuing digital badges as credentials for youth to demonstrate competencies gained in the summer. This experience spurred them to seek some way to start this work in their home city. Big Thought representatives took what they learned from Chicago back to their mayor, who endorsed the idea of replicating the work in Dallas; the lessons learned from Chicago became the springboard for an initiative called the Dallas City of Learning (DCOL). The initiative's efforts targeted high-poverty neighborhoods identified by the mayor's task force to eliminate poverty.

Big Thought, the City of Dallas, and DISD were the primary partners in the DCOL. Big Thought assumed several roles, including directly providing programs; funding programs through aligning and coordinating the funding efforts of local foundations and corporations; observing program quality by enlisting, training, and deploying a set of contractors to observe programs; offering PD by coordinating resources across several high-capacity OST organizations and offering them to all program providers; hosting networking meetings; identifying programs in communities by coordinating with neighborhood and faith-based organizations; forging partnerships among programs; fundraising; designing evaluations with higher education and DISD partners; overseeing the development of an online program locator; and reporting on outcomes. The city was also a direct program provider: Its Parks and Recreation, Library Departments, and Office of Arts and Culture provided programs in their facilities and the Mayor's Office hosted a youth employment program. The school district was a major program provider, providing multiple academic experiences for youth across the city. The district partnered with Big Thought on many of these programs to complement academic instruction with community-based arts provision, including programs funded by The Wallace Foundation as part of the NSLP.

Goals and Related Activities

The goal of DCOL was to increase access to and participation in summer opportunities among children and youth of all ages who lived in low-income neighborhoods that lacked many summer program opportunities; to improve the quality of existing programming; and to recognize the competencies that participants built through these experiences. To create a coordinated summer system, Big Thought identified existing summer programs in high-need neighborhoods and recruited them into the effort. The three partnering organizations also developed new in-person programs and created online opportunities; in some of these programs, participation could result in the awarding of a digital

> **Big Thought, the City of Dallas, and DISD were the primary partners in the DCOL.**

badge demonstrating an earned competency in a skill, such as a specific computer programming language. Though badging was a significant part of DCOL at the start, multiple interviewees noted that youth participation in the badging opportunities was lower than anticipated, and that focus waned over time.

To accomplish these tasks, Big Thought established a fundraising committee geared toward the private sector in the hopes of supplementing public funding. This effort, called the DCOL Champions Campaign, successfully raised millions of dollars, which supported the expansion of summer programming along with PD and technical assistance to improve the quality of programming.

Big Thought staff also aimed to provide new programming opportunities in underserved areas by attracting and supporting a new program to a neighborhood, by creating and supporting new partnerships among existing programs, or by a combination of the two approaches. Interviewees described how cultivating relationships in schools and in communities was crucial in learning about programs in high-need areas identified by the mayor's task force and recruiting these programs' leaders to be under the larger DCOL umbrella. For example, one interviewee described "a lot of door knocking, a lot of partner meetings" in various communities, and a specific targeting of churches, which often have free or low-cost programming for youth. Multiple interviewees offered another example of a partnership that arose from networking under the DCOL umbrella: The owner of a mall in a high-need area with hardly any summer offerings donated vacant space to be used for new summer programming, and Big Thought worked with local community groups to launch new programs in this free space.

[B]ig Thought established a fundraising committee geared toward the private sector in the hopes of supplementing public funding.

Types of Programs

DCOL offered a wide variety of opportunities during summer 2016; some were newly created as a result of DCOL efforts, others were preexisting. These opportunities included specialized activities and events along with programs focused on the following:

- visual arts, dance, and theater

- parks and recreation

- academics, reading, technology, and coding.

One specialized activity was a science, technology, engineering, and mathematics (STEM)-focused recreation vehicle retrofitted with three-dimensional printers, Lego robotics, and other advanced technology that traveled to different summer programs (e.g., church- or CBO-based) for the day. Specialized events included "turn-up" events, which were typically one-day happenings hosted by different entities. For instance, the Dallas Love Field Airport hosted a turn-up event in which youth visited the Frontier of Flight museum, toured the maintenance facility, and learned about the behind-the-scenes operations of the airport.

To expand awareness of program opportunities, DCOL contracted with an external vendor to develop an online program locator. The program locator was intended to allow families to find programs and Big Thought to analyze attendance data. Representatives from the various summer programs provided program information to Big Thought to get their programs listed on the locator website. Interviewees from Big Thought reported that they included all the programs they could identify in the locator—even high-cost programs (although leaders of high-cost programs were encouraged to offer scholarships).

Outcomes

Interviewees described their outcomes as (1) creating the new program locator, (2) improving program quality, and (3) serving more children and youth each successive summer. In total, there were approximately 25,000 youth involved in activities and/or programs at approximately 130 different DCOL sites in summer 2016, an increase in the overall number served.

Continuously improving the quality of individual summer programs was a significant aim of the DCOL. Big Thought staff worked in high-need communities to identify existing providers, assess program quality, and collaborate with local providers on how to create new programs or expand existing ones. Big Thought staff members developed a quality rubric to observe and evaluate programs across the city. All summer programs funded through Big Thought underwent an external observation and received feedback on their performance (funding coordinated by Big Thought served as an incentive to participate in observation). Big Thought staff used the data to identify common PD needs across programs in the city. For example, drawing from observations across many different programs, Big Thought staff members concluded that "dialogue" (i.e., students talking with one another) and "creative choice making" (i.e., the ability for youth to make meaningful choices about their work and activities) were areas of improvement for many summer programs across the city. Big Thought staff worked with program leaders individually and through workshops to provide support for embedding these opportunities into summer program activities.

UPDATE ON DALLAS CITY OF LEARNING

The 2019 DCOL impact report stated that the network's 700 community partner organizations offered 2,735 programs, 95 percent of which were free, and served a total of 68,303 students in summer 2019 (Edwards, 2019). As of November 2020, the DCOL website offered 860 summer learning opportunities, which consisted of both at-home learning activities and in-person experiences. DCOL programs spanned a variety of topics such as coding and games, community action, designing and making, earth and science, media, numbers, performance, sports and wellness, storytelling, work and career, and zoology. (Big Thought, undated; DCOL, undated)

Pittsburgh Summer 16: Dream! Explore! Do!

The seeds for Pittsburgh's coordinated network, Pittsburgh's Summer 16: Dream! Explore! Do!, were sown by a 2014 report commissioned by the mayor's Education Task Force, which recommended that the mayor become more involved in summer programming for youth. Subsequently, the inspiration for a collaborative effort focused on summer came directly from a Wallace Foundation Professional Learning Community conference held in Boston in October 2015. At the conference, representatives from Pittsburgh Public Schools (PPS), Allegheny Partners for Out-of-School Time (APOST—a partnership of funders, intermediaries, and providers dedicated to building a quality OST system in the county), and Allies for Children (a nonprofit entity advocating children's well-being in the county) participated in a presentation on their summer programming efforts, and the idea was then brought back to the mayor in Pittsburgh. Two meetings were called by the United Way of Southwestern Pennsylvania/APOST in December 2015, the first with program providers to get their input and support and the second with the mayor's office to get the mayor's support to launch a formal campaign.

Partners and Their Roles

The mayor signed on in February 2016, formally kicking off the collaborative work. Several meetings took place either monthly or biweekly throughout the early months of 2016—beginning with the first convening in February—with the following organizations:

- City of Pittsburgh

- City Department of Parks and Recreation

- Allies for Children

- The Sprout Fund

- Pittsburgh Public Schools

- Carnegie Library of Pittsburgh

- A+ Schools

- United Way of Southwestern Pennsylvania/Allegheny Partners for Out-of-School Time (APOST).

Each of these organizations brought unique assets to the coordinated work. For example, the mayor's team designed a logo, and Allies for Children engaged bloggers to publicize the work. The Sprout Fund commissioned a video about the coordinated network. APOST invited program providers to join its continuous improvement quality campaign and then complete a series of self-assessment and improvement steps designed by APOST.

Interviewees explained that they intentionally did not want to have an official leader for their initiative, although they had a de facto public-facing leader (the mayor) and multiple coordinating organizations. The mayor's office, APOST, and Allies for Children took turns hosting meetings, and multiple stakeholders from each organization would help set the agendas. Interviewees noted that this nonleader model was deliberate and part of the reason the collaboration worked well, although one interviewee did wonder whether the initiative would have been stronger with a clearly identified organization taking the day-to-day lead.

Goals and Related Activities

The resulting initiative, Pittsburgh's Summer 16: Dream! Explore! Do! (or in short, Summer 16) aimed to spread awareness about summer programs for youth in Pittsburgh, with the mayor setting a goal of serving 16,000 youth, modeled after the mayoral goal set in Boston. Youth participation had not been tracked well in the past, but most agreed it had been fewer than 16,000 children and youth. The general perception in Pittsburgh was that there were lots of summer opportunities for city youth, but parents were not as aware of them as they could have been. Many of the leaders of this work had heard about or knew of programs that had been canceled because of low enrollment, leading some Pittsburgh stakeholders to believe there was more program supply than demand.

Consequently, Summer 16 focused on making it easier for parents to learn about programs and events as a way to increase youth participation in available programming, with a secondary emphasis on closing income-based participation gaps. As one interviewee explained, "I felt like this year our goal was 'let's just make a big splash' to get parents to think about summer programming for their children." She continued, "[o]ur goal was getting to our number of 16,000." The Pittsburgh initiative met this goal; more than 16,000 children and youth engaged in summer activities and programs in summer 2016. Initiative leaders could not discern participants by income or neighborhood, however, to understand whether access to summer programs had improved for those experiencing poverty.

Types of Programs

There were many programs available that summer, such as the following:

- Learn and Earn, the mayor's youth employment program, which placed youth in summer jobs at roughly 375 organizations

- Summer Dreamers Academy, hosted by PPS, which served 2,190 students with academic and enrichment programming

- programs run by the Parks and Recreation department, such as swimming, park ranger programs, and a mobile Art Cart program

- programs run by the Carnegie Library of Pittsburgh

- programs run by CBOs (e.g., the YMCA).

[S]ummer 16 focused on making it easier for parents to learn about programs and events as a way to increase youth participation in available programming.

To help cover marketing and promotional costs, Summer 16 raised $15,000 from a local foundation. There were kickoff events and media coverage leading up to the summer, highlighting the Summer 16 website as the main vehicle for parents to learn about summer programs. The main summer kickoff event, which was held in March and attended by more than 100 people and held at the Carnegie Library of Pittsburgh–East Liberty branch, was the premier event of the initiative: The mayor gave a speech, the Allegheny County Executive participated, and local media covered the event. One interviewee described it this way: "At that press event, we wanted kids there, we wanted teachers, program [provider]s there—we just wanted a ton of people there to celebrate and launch this Summer 16 effort."

Outcomes

The main product of this network was a new website—built on an existing APOST database but designed and hosted by the city—that featured a calendar of events and a program locator, which allowed the user to select the type of program of interest and get matches for programs in the county. The goal was to spread the word about all the different opportunities while promoting the importance of summer opportunities to the public. As one interviewee said, "[i]t was a communications effort." Any program could provide its details to be entered into the online program locator (they could do this themselves or an APOST staff member would do it for them); interviewees from APOST explained that there were no exclusion criteria related to the cost of a program, though one interviewee mentioned that several individual programs only served youth from low-income families. To gauge participation in summer programming across the city, APOST requested attendance data from providers at the end of the summer.

Interviewees described the following outcomes of Summer 16: The city surpassed its goal of 16,000 participating youth. Interviewed program leaders noted that they had large increases in applications from 2015 to 2016 and speculated that this might be a result of increased parental awareness created by the Summer 16 initiative. In addition, some interviewees said that the initiative deepened connections among program providers through the meetings held among the network leaders. For instance, some interviewees explained that when their program slots were filled, they were able to direct youth and their families to other programs that they knew about because of the collaborative work.

Washington, D.C., Summer Strong

A desire to coordinate government agencies charged with serving high-need communities and to generate data on services provided during the summer drove the collaborative summer work in Washington, D.C. The 2015 dissolution of the D.C. Trust, a nonprofit that previously collected and tracked data related to summer programs, resulted in city leaders facing an information void. Without this coordinator, they lacked knowledge about constituents' access to and participation in summer opportunities and were unable to answer core questions from agency leadership about programming and services in summer 2015. To fill this gap, the mayor launched a city-level collaborative effort titled "Summer Strong."

Partners and Their Roles

In the District of Columbia, the mayor controls the public schools, and she tasked the deputy mayor of education to coordinate the Summer Strong efforts.

Several agencies played a prominent role in Summer Strong, including the following:

- Office of the Deputy Mayor for Education (DME), which coordinated efforts for Summer Strong and coordinated the district's mandatory summer learning programs

- Department of Parks and Recreation, which ran traditional recreational youth programming (103 camps total) and held activities, such as midnight basketball tournaments

- Department of Employee Services, which ran the Summer Youth Employment Program that had roughly 13,000 participants in 2016

- Office of the Deputy Mayor for Health and Human Services, which had an initiative called Safer, Stronger D.C. Community Partnerships

- Department of Housing and Community Development, which provided programming for children and families living in public housing

- Metropolitan Police Department, which supported other agencies' events and hosted community festivals called "Beat the Streets"

- Office of the Deputy Mayor for Public Safety and Justice, which ran a violent crime victim stabilization effort that linked families to resources, including programming for youth

- Office of the State Superintendent of Education, which offered a free meal program for youth 18 years old and under.

Many of these agencies had already worked together on a year-round basis, so they had a solid network on which to build Summer Strong.

Goals and Related Activities

The tagline for Summer Strong was "fit days, safe nights, strong communities." DME developed four citywide goals to drive the Summer Strong vision and work:

1. Reach residents.

2. Focus resources in high-need areas.

3. Engage entire families.

4. Build communities.

The tagline for Summer Strong was "fit days, safe nights, strong communities."

Resources were targeted toward neighborhoods that were more likely to see increased crime rates during the summer months. Individual agencies were tasked with creating their own goals, metrics, and desired outcomes for each of the four citywide goals with the following guiding questions:

- Reach residents: How will you maximize your reach to touch more residents?

- Focus resources: How will you focus your resources in the target police service areas?

- Engage families: How will you create opportunities that engage multiple generations?

- Build community: How will you leverage your work to build and strengthen community?

Representatives from the departments met biweekly starting in the winter and continuing through the summer to present their strategies, identify gaps in services, and strategize about how to deliver coordinated services to high-need communities. One interviewee explained the initiative's purpose as follows:

> Summer Strong brings them all together, helps map out where they provide services, and then find where they have voids in the city where they might have a specific age group not being served that Parks and Rec doesn't have a program for or DCPS [District of Columbia Public Schools] isn't serving.

Representatives also attended steering committee meetings to report data to higher-level government leaders, including deputy mayors and sometimes the mayor; further discussions and planning occurred in these meetings as well.

Types of Programs

The Washington, D.C., initiative differed from those in the study's other three cities by focusing on serving neighborhoods and families in them rather than concentrating mainly on youth participation. As a result, Summer Strong coordinated, tracked, and advertised a variety of programs and services:

Resources were targeted toward neighborhoods that were more likely to see increased crime rates during the summer months.

- academic summer programs provided by public and charter schools

- recreational summer programs offered by Parks and Recreation and Housing and Community Development

- youth employment programs

- community events, such as basketball nights or festivals

- summer meal services.

Outcomes

Each agency documented and reported on the status of its activities and their outcomes at the end of the summer. We highlight some of these noted outcomes:

- **Reach Residents.** The city used a multipronged approach to inform families about summer opportunities: organizers issued a spring press release; distributed information kits in the wards (neighborhoods); and developed a website that allowed families to locate events and programs, including midnight basketball, neighborhood movie nights, education programs for students, such as distribution sites, and recreational summer programs. In the first summer, about 1,500 residents visited the online summer activity finder; 73 percent of those users went to the website multiple times. Some agencies also shared information through social media. For instance, the Department of Parks and Recreation tweeted about its events. The city also received a grant to procure a text-messaging service based on the citywide calendar that residents could sign up for to be notified about programs in their areas; however, take-up in the first year was relatively low.

- **Focus Resources.** Each agency targeted resources and activities to the highest-need police service areas (i.e., high-crime neighborhoods). For example, D.C. Public Schools and the Department of Employment Services targeted recruitment for its summer programs to schools within the targeted police service areas; both agencies increased the number of youth served from those areas of the city.

- **Engage Families.** Each agency enacted strategies to engage whole families and not just children. For instance, five of the 11 summer service providers on public housing properties in the designated police service areas sponsored activities for the entire family. The public schools held parental engagement meetings once a week at seven of nine of its summer sites serving students in kindergarten through seventh grade.

- **Build Community.** Each agency enacted strategies to ensure that programs served or provided benefits to all members of the community. For instance, public libraries provided summer reading programs across all age ranges and saw a significant increase in adult participation.

In addition to the citywide data gathered on summer program opportunities and participation, interviewees noted that constituents described positive differences in the neighborhoods as a result of these efforts. One interviewee recalled a conversation with a constituent:

> She said, "Since you all have been doing this work, it's so much more peace[ful] in our neighborhood." When she talked about peace, she said, "It's a lot more quiet, and [there's] a lot more to do in terms of when we look up [programs on the website], there's an opportunity, there's some type of event going on, or a mobile unit in the neighborhood so people can get whatever resource they might need." That's what we offer, especially during the summer. We offer positive opportunities and positive resources and opportunities to engage residents.

[I]nterviewees noted that constituents described positive differences in the neighborhoods as a result of these efforts.

UPDATE ON WASHINGTON, D.C., SUMMER STRONG

Washington, D.C., continued its focus on summer offerings, which are now coordinated by the Office of Out of School Time Grants and Youth Outcomes (OST Office), located in the DME, and features an increased focus on opportunities for children and youth. The OST office leads Learn24, a network of high-quality afterschool and summer opportunities for District of Columbia children and youth, informed by the mayor's Commission on Out of School Time Grants and Youth Outcomes (DME, undated). In April 2019, the OST Office awarded $4.8 million in Summer Strong grants to 56 organizations that provide districtwide summer programming. This funding allowed more than 5,000 District of Columbia youth access to free or low-cost safe and enriching opportunities to learn and grow during the summer months (DME, 2019). As of November 2020, the program finder listed 74 OST programs and a long list of focus areas, such as academic support, arts, computer/technology, environmental education, graphic design, health, life skills, mentoring, sports, and STEM. The district continued accepting applications for Summer Strong 2021 grants.

CHAPTER THREE

Progress and Challenges

I n the first section of this report, we described indicators of successful coordinated networks. Common indicators (which can also be considered enablers of success) across the networks described in the literature are **shared vision**, **strong leadership**, **coordinated action**, **funding for sustainability**, and **collecting diagnostic data**. In this section, we consider the progress made by the coordinated networks on each of these indicators in turn, as well as challenges they reported facing during their early years of coordination.

Shared Vision

Each of the cities established a collective vision of what it hoped to accomplish. Although all focused on summer opportunities, the visions' scopes and associated goals differed. These visions coalesced with few challenges and emerged from

- perceived need

- the availability of an opportunity

- local context

- the capabilities of the organizations involved in the effort.

In three of the cities, these visions developed out of an agreement among key organizations about what could and should be accomplished. In each of these cases, the mayor's support for that vision was considered key to moving forward and galvanizing other partners to participate. In Washington, D.C., the vision was set by the mayor and deputy mayors. It was then incorporated into the ongoing work of city agencies. In the other cities, the vision was set by the partners, and the mayor's office promoted the vision, along with participation goals. For example, in Boston, the mayor's goal of serving 10,000 youth by summer 2017 prompted additional programs to join the quality network.

Establishing a vision and obtaining buy-in was not challenging in these cities. As noted earlier in this report, these networks had been addressing summer programming for several years: Boston, Dallas, and Pittsburgh had participated in the NSLP, which had brought citywide attention to the topic. This preexisting foundation might have made it easier for these cities to establish a common vision for how to continue and extend that work. Washington, D.C., did not participate in the NSLP, but its networking initiative was driven by the mayor, which allowed for fairly smooth vision-setting and launch processes.

Although the overarching vision in each city remained consistent and shared, strategies shifted as leaders learned from the work. For instance, in Dallas, the emphasis on digital badging lessened over time.

Strong Leadership

The frameworks call out two ways that leadership matters to these efforts. First, the leader(s) of the initiative must have the right capabilities and be credible among stakeholders to galvanize support. Second, the initiative must have the support of key leaders in the community for their organizations to prioritize this work.

We observed a variety of leadership models (Figure 3.1). In Pittsburgh, there was an explicit distribution of leadership among APOST, the school district, the mayor's office, and other key CBOs. Each of the stakeholders had the expertise and the influence to raise awareness of summer opportunities among their own constituents. In Boston and Dallas, an intermediary organization served as the key organizer and facilitating entity of the work

Although the overarching vision in each city remained consistent and shared, strategies shifted as leaders learned from the work.

alongside the city, school district, and summer program providers. Each of these organizations had the capability, experience, and network to lead the effort. In Washington, D.C., the mayor and deputy mayors were considered the leaders of the coordination effort, and the Department of Education was charged with facilitating the work of the partner agencies. All four cities had a functioning leadership model, but a small number of interviewees was critical of the structure in each city; some wished for a larger role for another organization or questioned the unique value-add of the lead organization. We also observed that the two networks coordinated by intermediaries were further along in their quality-improvement efforts, which might have been facilitated by their fundraising success—the dollars that they raised supported such activities as observing program instruction, surveying teachers about students' SEL competencies, providing tailored evaluation reports to individual programs, and hosting PD sessions.

In all of the cities, the mayors were strong champions and engaged leaders of the networks. There were no challenges reported in

FIGURE 3.1
Leadership Models of Coordinated Networks in Study

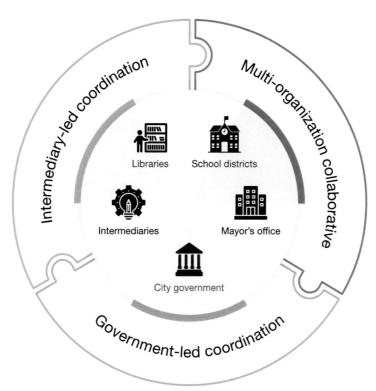

garnering this support. Perhaps in Pittsburgh and Dallas, the mayors saw this opportunity as a way to help students, given their limited roles in formal education. Conversely, the Boston and District of Columbia mayors led education in their cities and perhaps clearly saw the value in continuing to provide academically and personally enriching and safe programs in the summer. Across the four cities, interviewees described mayors as enhancing the community's attention to summer programming, getting the media involved, influencing funders, and commanding the respect and diligence of the organizations and individuals involved in the day-to-day work. As one put it:

> Definitely the mayor's office . . . we have to have that support from the [mayor's office] in order to make it a priority. They're the key right there. Without them, it's just not going to get done. You have to have that pressure from the [mayor's office] to get people to sit up and do something.

Coordinated Action

Citywide efforts depend on the coordination of multiple stakeholders, which requires establishing structures for coordination and garnering active participation of primary and secondary stakeholders. These cases demonstrate that different organizational structures—such as intragovernmental department coordination, intermediary-led coordination, and multi-organization collaboratives—can be effective. Across all cities, coordination around summer was built on prior collaborative efforts. And each of the networks communicated a consistent and coordinated message to parents, program providers, and youth about the importance and benefits of summer programs.

In Boston, Dallas, and Pittsburgh, network leaders wanted to improve the quality of summer programming and collect data from programs to measure progress toward youth participation goals. To garner cooperation of summer program providers, network leaders highlighted the benefits of network participation: PD opportunities, data about program quality, and (in some cases) funding. Some network leaders asked providers to sign pledges committing to participating in network activities. In Dallas, network leaders created new, high-quality video and photographs of summer programming that providers could use in marketing

Citywide efforts depend on the coordination of multiple stakeholders, which requires establishing structures for coordination and garnering active participation of primary and secondary stakeholders.

their programs in exchange for program data. Dallas leaders also hosted an annual meeting after the summer for the provider community, featuring city leaders, the presentation of data from the summer, and opportunities for networking and learning.

However, not all program providers fully bought in to the coordinated effort. Some providers wanted more benefits for their own organizations, asserting that funding was better spent on programming than on system-level efforts or that they could not see enough benefits for providers. As one provider noted:

> I think the big challenge is that they have not shown what the benefit is for partners to be part of [the network]. We don't get any kind of data, or "hey 80 percent of the people in this program also go to this program." It hasn't shown why we would want to be part of it.

Another interviewee described the challenge of ensuring that all partnering organizations had the most-recent information and plans during busy times of implementation:

> Which I think is sometimes one of the drawbacks [of a coordinated network], where if they get too far ahead, or head in a different direction than [us], it creates some division.

Funding for Sustainability

Apart from funding for the programs themselves, coordinated citywide efforts require sustained financial investments to support the work. Each of the cities had a specific scope with different financial requirements. In Pittsburgh and Washington, D.C., the cost of the coordinated efforts was primarily personnel time. Given the demands on leaders and staff in partnering organizations, these opportunity costs were significant. Prioritizing the work on summer required a shift away from other activities. Each of these cities also received a small donation for advertising and outreach ($15,000 or less from a local foundation, for example).

Each of the cities had a specific scope with different financial requirements.

The visions of Boston and Dallas officials to aggressively improve quality and create new programs in low-income neighborhoods, respectively, meant that the need for external finances was greater.

Leaders worked to raise money to support both the funding of some programs directly and the cost of operating the coordinated effort, which involved collecting data, creating a database, providing PD, and more. One interviewee thought that raising money for the network was easier than raising money for individual programs because funders understood that they were investing in improving an entire system of programs:

> Whenever . . . we're saying make an investment at a systems level so we can bring a comprehensive, searchable, one-stop place for kids where we can build quality and seats for kids; where we can target technical assistance in the places we need it most . . . whenever we're raising money at that systems level . . . we're able to raise substantially more money than when we're trying to raise money for a particular program or initiative.

But interviewees also raised concerns about the sustainability of funding, particularly as their networks grew. In Boston, expanded demand and reduced resources caused a move from research partners conducting external observations to a lower-cost method: training program leaders to observe peer programs. Interviewees noted upsides and downsides to this shift. Some were concerned that it was more difficult to guarantee interrater reliability (i.e., that all raters would rate the same practice the same way on the observation instrument). Other interviewees recognized that, by being trained on the observation tool, the providers were deepening their understanding of the underlying quality practices measured.

Collecting Diagnostic Data

Collecting data enables shared accountability, quality improvement, and communication and messaging to stakeholders. As discussed earlier, measuring the impact of programs in communities is a complex and complicated endeavor, requiring substantial resources if the goal is to untangle causation. In most cases, understanding whether both participation and program quality are improving is sufficient for parents' and other stakeholders' needs. Boston measured child and youth outcomes beyond participation; the other communities in the study chose not to.

Each city had goals for, and attempted to measure, participation in programming. This is more challenging than it might seem. Although the cities all estimated the number of youth attending each program, these youth were likely counted more than once in the aggregate, citywide. For example, if a young person attended a dance program in June and a Parks and Recreation swimming program in July, there was no way the systems in these cities could determine that it was the same person attending both programs.

Stemming from the scope of its goals, Washington, D.C., also tracked adult participation in programs, number of meals served, and crime rates in police service areas.

In cities where improving program quality was a goal of the systemwide effort, organizers based their assessments of program improvement on observations of programming. Network leaders conducted the observations in one of three ways: (1) doing the work themselves, (2) contracting with local researchers, or (3) using a peer approach by which program leaders observed each other's programs using a standard observation tool. Boston also implemented pre-post surveys of youth and instructors to gather data about program quality and youth outcomes.

In Boston, leaders used data to motivate program leaders to participate in the network and to drive community interest in summer. Boston leaders collected data on youth enrollment, attendance, and SEL outcomes; these data were reported to individual providers, who received their own results benchmarked to city averages. These data formed the basis of continuous improvement support throughout the year. Multiple programs came together for PD sessions to discuss practice within a peer-learning community and to strategize about common challenges, such as developing intentional programming, strengthening attendance, finding qualified staff, and managing facilities and transportation. These sessions had strong attendance, and program providers valued the data and learning that came through membership in the summer quality network.

Cities also reported challenges in collecting, reporting, and using data for continuous improvement processes. As noted, each city wanted to track progress toward the goal of serving more children and youth each summer but was unable to get a precise count. In Dallas and Pittsburgh, getting programs to report enrollment data was also challenging, both in terms of incentivizing the programs to do it and in terms of the personnel time needed to transcribe reported numbers into spreadsheets. Furthermore, gathering, analyzing, and reporting data require investing in staff with the expertise to do these tasks. In Boston, where data-sharing is core to the network, Boston After School & Beyond employs a full-time data analyst who has an advanced degree and training in data analysis.

> [G]athering, analyzing, and reporting data require investing in staff with the expertise to do these tasks.

Boston network leaders attempted to connect youth data from summer programs to youth data from their school district, and—according to interviewees—were unable to get a match for roughly two-thirds of their population because of issues with student names (e.g., hyphenated last names, duplicate names, misspelled names). The network wanted to see whether there was a connection between summer program participation and academic outcomes. That is an ambitious goal necessitating expertise and technology, as well as funding for both. If a network is tracking participation in summer programs and, at the same time, helping programs improve quality, it is likely setting itself up to measure achievement of the most common goal of these networks: increasing access to quality summer program opportunities.

CHAPTER FOUR

Conclusions and Recommendations for Other Cities

The summer time frame has always provided an opportunity to focus on children and youth who need support; currently, there is a greater focus on (and more funding for) summer programs as the nation turns to addressing the impacts of the global pandemic. The additional funding is for the 2021–2023 time frame, allowing school districts, community organizations, city leaders, and others the resources and time to build and strengthen coordinated networks to promote access to quality summer programs. This report addresses the call of the National Academies of Sciences, Engineering, and Medicine's consensus study on summer opportunities to improve citywide coordination to ensure equitable summertime experiences for all children and youth:

> Summer provides a unique window of opportunity to engage families and leverage the strengths of those families, the communities in which they live, and other stakeholders to improve the well-being of children and youth. Better collaboration

and coordination among these parties are needed to identify and prioritize high-quality summertime experiences, with special attention to the needs of children and youth who currently lack these opportunities. (National Academies of Sciences, Engineering, and Medicine, 2019b, p. 1)

In each of the cities we studied, organizations had been focused on the importance of summer services for youth and communities and had experience collaborating with one another. As a result, galvanizing a coordinated effort around summer was a relatively easy next step, particularly with mayoral support. Mayors served as strong and visible leaders of this work and individual organizations provided skilled leadership, building networks based on established relationships. We also found that different organizational structures—such as intragovernmental department coordination, intermediary-led coordination, and multi-organization collaboratives—can be effective. Arguably, the intermediary-led networks were further along in their quality improvement efforts, perhaps because of their fundraising success.

> Arguably, the intermediary-led networks were further along in their quality improvement efforts, perhaps because of their fundraising success.

The goals of the coordinated efforts varied: raising awareness about summer programming in the community, improving program quality, increasing access to and participation in summer programs, neighborhood safety, and community engagement.

Reflecting on the common indicators of progress, we find that the coordinated networks developed shared visions fairly easily, demonstrated that different leadership models can be successful, coordinated activities across organizations, raised various levels of funding (demonstrating what is possible), and used data to measure increases in access to programs and the quality of that programming.

We also identified additional nuances not noted in the literature we reviewed. Although the literature focuses on the importance of developing a shared vision, we noted that leaders of the networks we studied also set goals and strategies that capitalized on their structure. These were both *authentic*, meaning that the goals were important for their community, but were also *achievable* because of the leadership structure. For example, in Washington, D.C., leaders could set a goal to reduce summer crime rates because the mayor led the Summer Strong initiative and had authority over the police department. We also found that engaging the program providers in network activities was not straightforward. In any network, leaders might want or need to engage direct service providers in coordinating services to better meet needs, improving quality, or participating in other network activities. We identified ways to get this buy-in that might be useful for others building networks.

Through their efforts, the networks succeeded in raising awareness of summer opportunities throughout their cities and providing information to families about specific programs. In Boston, Dallas, and Pittsburgh, the number of children and youth participating increased. Some new programs were developed in high-need areas. In general, there were signs that more attention was being paid to summer opportunities by funders and policymakers as well (e.g., funders' willingness to support summer programs that were part of a quality network). Although the focus was on youth programming in most of the cities, network leaders in Washington, D.C., also provided programs to adults in the community. Boston, Dallas, and Pittsburgh leaders also developed continuous improvement models and supported individual programs' quality development. It is also worth noting that, to our knowledge, all these collaborative efforts remained strong through summer 2019 and have continued their work—including supporting providers as they pivoted to virtual program options during the coronavirus pandemic.

Even with these successes, establishing and maintaining buy-in for collaborative work requires ongoing effort. Some individual program providers questioned network leadership and fundraising models, saying they saw themselves as pitted against the networks for local foundation funding. Sustainability was a challenge, causing some networks to rethink their approaches to quality improvement efforts, which can be costly. It also took considerable effort to keep partners informed and moving in the same direction. Despite the networks, programs still faced perennial obstacles, such as finding qualified staff, safe buildings, and reliable transportation. However, these challenges did not prevent the networks from continuing. Program providers appreciated many benefits from these coordinated efforts, including shared data and funding.

Program providers appreciated many benefits from these coordinated efforts, including shared data and funding.

The cities' experiences suggest that citywide coordination among youth-focused organizations could help increase awareness of, attention to, participation in, and improvements to summer learning programs.

Recommendations

Using our observations of the work in these four cities, we provide recommendations for organizational leaders in other cities who want to develop or strengthen coordinated networks focused on summer programming, highlighting the ways in which the networks we studied strove to overcome the challenges noted. Our recommendations focus on launching a coordinated network, setting and achieving goals, promoting equity, and gathering and using data to assess progress. These recommendations are targeted to those wanting to increase participation in quality summer opportunities but might also be relevant to other types of networks.

Launching a Coordinated Network

Set a broad vision that allows for strategic evolution. As noted earlier, the vision for summer programs remained consistent in each of the cities; however, strategies for achieving these visions shifted. As some networks matured, they spent less time on improving access to programming and more time on the quality of programming. Others moved away from specific activities, such as competency-based badging, without abandoning the vision of increasing participation in quality summer opportunities. We recommend adopting this flexibility as a network matures and its members learn more about the needs of its particular locale.

Garner mayoral support for the citywide effort. One strategy used by all network leaders was involving the city's mayor. Mayors set communitywide goals for student participation in summer programs, asked to be kept apprised of progress, made summer programming a mayoral initiative, assigned staff to take on such tasks as creating and hosting program locators on city websites, and made public statements about the importance of summer programming. Interviewees described how mayoral involvement brought attention and funding to summer programs and maintained internal buy-in among network partners. Mayors in these cities motivated the work and kept it on the community agenda.

Leverage the experiences of past local coordination efforts.
The efforts we studied were built on established relationships.
A variety of organizations made this work possible in our study
cities, notably intermediaries, philanthropic organizations, CBOs
and other nonprofits, research organizations, local school districts, and city and county agencies. Different types of organizations took the lead in our studied cities. An intermediary, such
as Boston After School & Beyond or Big Thought, might make
a strong lead in a given city, as might a city agency or advocacy
organization in another. In general, we recommend reflecting
on the established relationships in a given context and modeling
new networks on those that have worked to address other social
needs. We also recommend expanding established relationships.
Interviewees recommended involving agencies that might not typically be at the table but might have established connections with
families, such as divisions of homeless services in county agencies.

Setting and Achieving Goals

**Align the goals and strategies to the organizational structure
of the coordinated effort.** As noted, we found that different
organizational structure—such as intragovernmental department coordination, intermediary-led coordination, and multi-
organization collaboratives—can be effective. In some cases, the
cities capitalized on a given structure to accomplish goals that
could only be supported by that particular structure. For instance,
in Washington, D.C., which established intragovernmental department coordination, the city was able to target residents of all ages
and use strategies that required city government leverage because
the mayor asked the leaders of schools, human services, the police
department, and parks and recreation to meet every other week
from January through the summer to set goals and report on
progress. It would have taken much more effort in the other cities
to involve these other departments—it might have been possible,
but the structure in the District of Columbia made it feasible.

Align strategies to goals for summer programming. In addition
to considering how the structure of a citywide effort supports
goals and strategies, the goals and strategies themselves should
align. For example, if a citywide goal is to promote greater access
to quality summer programming opportunities, there should
be coordinated city work aimed at determining and/or increasing the number of participants *and* improving the quality of

programming. If the goal is to increase access for populations that have not historically had it, communities need to measure progress by neighborhood, income level, or another demographic of interest rather than overall increases in participation.

Carefully consider strategies and the resources needed to implement them well. Each strategy adopted requires a set of conditions that are necessary to ensure robust implementation. For instance, adopting a program locator requires (1) technological expertise, (2) the ability to populate the database with program information each year, (3) sufficient community awareness to make it a valued resource, and (4) sufficient resources to invest in development, incentives for providers, and marketing. Without meeting these conditions, implementation could fail and might not be worth the investment of time and resources. A strategy built on shared data requires staff and partners with analytic and measurement expertise; an established set of shared measurement tools; a set of shared, desired outcomes; data systems that securely store data; a process for analyzing and reporting data to partners; and support for providers to help them understand and use data to drive program improvement.

Promoting Equity

Consider targeting efforts to neighborhoods with the greatest need. Two of the cities we studied focused their efforts on specific neighborhoods, and interviewees there described being able to develop partnerships and programs in areas with the most need (e.g., those with high poverty or crime rates). Similarly, another city began with a small set of programs as a pilot and expanded across the city over time. Focusing on neighborhoods where residents and youth are facing the most disadvantages (e.g., areas of high poverty or crime), might address the most-pressing needs in a more comprehensive manner than could be accomplished if tackling an entire city at once. Developing more programs in areas of high need also might reduce the necessity of finding low-cost, reliable transportation for children and youth to leave these neighborhoods for program opportunities. Increasing the size and quality of small programs in these neighborhoods might be a good starting point. There might also be vacant spaces (such as empty malls or abandoned schools) in these neighborhoods that cities or property owners could donate for summer programming.

Gathering and Using Data to Consider Progress

Determine how to assess progress early in the process. We also recommend developing an evaluation plan early in the process, specifying the data needed to assess achievement of goals, and ensuring that staffing and data structures are in place to support the plan (Yoo, Whitaker, and McCombs, 2019). To varying degrees, some of the cities struggled to determine the extent to which they were meeting their goals. If, for example, a goal is to increase participation in summer opportunities, it is important to determine how that will be measured. It might require establishing mechanisms for collecting attendance data across programs from year to year. Program attendance and other data could be used not only for tracking goal attainment but also for continuous improvement purposes. If a goal is to improve access to quality programs, leaders of citywide efforts should develop mechanisms for defining quality and continuously assessing and improving programs. Three of the cities we focused on strove to improve quality, and each made impressive strides toward this goal. In the cities with the most-advanced work on quality improvement, network leaders had raised significant new funding. These dollars supported such activities as observing program instruction, surveying teachers about students' SEL competencies, providing tailored evaluation reports to individual programs, and hosting PD sessions. When determining who will collect and analyze data on program quality, consider partnering with local research organizations or universities (as one network did), building that capacity within one of the leading network organizations (as was the case in another city), or creating the capacity among program leaders for peer evaluation.

> We also recommend developing an evaluation plan early in the process, specifying the data needed to assess achievement of goals, and ensuring that staffing and data structures are in place to support the plan.

Create incentives to ensure provider buy-in. Citywide efforts often require program provider buy-in. In some cases, the organizations leading these efforts are also providers themselves. Those not part of the leadership team might be called on to deliver data, expand programs, and participate in quality-improvement efforts. We recommend adopting the strategies that our interviewees found successful in incentivizing individual program providers to join the networks, such as offering (1) funding, (2) participation and outcome data reports to individual providers for their own use, (3) PD and networking activities, and (4) videos or high-resolution photographs of program activities that could be used in subsequent marketing efforts. In addition, some networks asked providers to sign pledges committing to participate in data-sharing or other network activities with specific tasks and due dates. Achieving program provider buy-in helps the network leaders measure progress toward meeting their goals and helps the programs themselves improve their quality.

ABBREVIATIONS

ACT	Achieve-Connect-Thrive
APOST	Allegheny Partners for Out-of-School Time
BPS	Boston Public Schools
CBO	community-based organization
CGLR	Campaign for Grade-Level Reading
DCOL	Dallas City of Learning
DISD	Dallas Independent School District
DME	Office of the Deputy Mayor for Education (Washington, D.C.)
NSLA	National Summer Learning Association
NSLP	National Summer Learning Project
OST	out-of-school time
PD	professional development
PPS	Pittsburgh Public Schools
SEL	social-emotional learning
STEM	science, technology, engineering, and mathematics

REFERENCES

Allegheny Partners for Out-of-School Time, "Program Finder," webpage, undated. As of November 11, 2020:
https://www.afterschoolpgh.org

APOST—*See* Allegheny Partners for Out-of-School Time.

Augustine, Catherine H., Jennifer Sloan McCombs, John F. Pane, Heather L. Schwartz, Jonathan Schweig, Andrew McEachin, and Kyle Siler-Evans, *Learning from Summer: Effects of Voluntary Summer Learning Programs on Low-Income Urban Youth*, Santa Monica, Calif.: RAND Corporation, RR-1557-WF, 2016. As of October 24, 2020:
https://www.rand.org/pubs/research_reports/RR1557.html

Augustine, Catherine H., Jennifer Sloan McCombs, Heather L. Schwartz, and Laura Zakaras, *Getting to Work on Summer Learning: Recommended Practices for Success*, 1st ed., Santa Monica, Calif.: RAND Corporation, RR-366-WF, 2013. As of October 24, 2020:
https://www.rand.org/pubs/research_reports/RR366.html

Augustine, Catherine H., and Lindsey E. Thompson, *Making Summer Last: Integrating Summer Programming into Core District Priorities and Operations*, Santa Monica, Calif.: RAND Corporation, RR-2038-WF, 2017. As of October 24, 2020:
https://www.rand.org/pubs/research_reports/RR2038.html

———, *Getting Support for Summer Learning: How Federal, State, City, and District Policies Affect Summer Learning Programs*, Santa Monica, Calif.: RAND Corporation, RR-2347-WF, 2020. As of October 24, 2020:
https://www.rand.org/pubs/research_reports/RR2347.html

Big Thought, "Dallas City of Learning," webpage, undated. As of November 11, 2020:
https://www.bigthought.org/who-we-are/our-programs/dallas-city-of-learning/

Bodilly, Susan J., and Catherine H. Augustine, *Revitalizing Arts Education Through Community-Wide Coordination*, Santa Monica, Calif.: RAND Corporation, MG-702-WF, 2008. As of October 24, 2019:
https://www.rand.org/pubs/monographs/MG702.html

Bodilly, Susan J., Jennifer Sloan McCombs, Nathan Orr, Ethan Scherer, Louay Constant, and Daniel Gershwin, *Hours of Opportunity*, Vol. 1, *Lessons from Five Cities on Building Systems to Improve After-School, Summer School, and Other Out-of-School-Time Programs*, Santa Monica, Calif.: RAND Corporation, MG-1037-WF, 2010. As of April 12, 2021:
https://www.rand.org/pubs/monographs/MG1037.html

Boston After School & Beyond, "Achieve-Connect-Thrive (ACT) Skills Framework: A Framework for Success," webpage, undated. As of October 24, 2019:
https://bostonbeyond.org/approach/skills/actframework/

———, *Summer Debrief and Celebration 2019: Ten Years in the Making*, Boston, Mass., April 2020. As of November 11, 2020:
https://bostonbeyond.org/wp-content/uploads/2020/04/
5th-Quarter-Data-Debrief-10-Year-Anniversary.pdf

Campaign for Grade-Level Reading, *Toward Closing the Gap(s)*, Washington, D.C., June 2017. As of October 24, 2019:
http://gradelevelreading.net/wp-content/uploads/2017/06/
TowardClosingTheGap_Final.pdf

CGLR—*See* Campaign for Grade-Level Reading.

Dallas City of Learning, website, undated. As of November 11, 2020:
https://dallascityoflearning.org/info/

DCOL—*See* Dallas City of Learning.

DME—*See* Office of the Deputy Mayor for Education (D.C.).

Edwards, Alex, *Impact Report: Dallas City of Learning Impacted 68K Students with Its Educational Programs This Summer,* Dallas: Dallas Innovates, December 2, 2019. As of November 11, 2020:
https://dallasinnovates.com/impact-report-dallas-city-of-learning-impacted-68k-students-with-its-learning-programs-this-summer/

Henig, Jeffrey R., Carolyn J. Riehl, David M. Houston, Michael A. Rebell, and Jessica R. Wolff, *Collective Impact and the New Generation of Cross-Sector Collaborations for Education: A Nationwide Scan,* New York: Teachers College, Columbia University, March 2016. As of October 24, 2019:
https://www.wallacefoundation.org/knowledge-center/Documents/Collective-Impact-and-the-New-Generation-of-Cross-Sector-Collaboration-for-Education.pdf

Kania, John, and Mark Kramer, "Essentials of Social Innovation: Collective Impact," *Stanford Social Innovation Review,* Winter 2011, pp. 36–41. As of October 24, 2019:
https://ssir.org/articles/entry/collective_impact

McCombs, Jennifer Sloan, Catherine H. Augustine, John F. Pane, and Jonathan Schweig, *Every Summer Counts: A Longitudinal Analysis of Outcomes from the National Summer Learning Project,* Santa Monica, Calif.: RAND Corporation, RR-3201-WF, 2020. As of January 28, 2021:
https://www.rand.org/pubs/research_reports/RR3201.html

McCombs, Jennifer Sloan, John F. Pane, Catherine H. Augustine, Heather L. Schwartz, Paco Martorell, and Laura Zakaras, *Ready for Fall? Near-Term Effects of Voluntary Summer Learning Programs on Low-Income Students' Learning Opportunities and Outcomes,* Santa Monica, Calif.: RAND Corporation, RR-815-WF, 2014. As of October 24, 2019:
https://www.rand.org/pubs/research_reports/RR815.html

National Academies of Sciences, Engineering, and Medicine, *Shaping Summertime Experiences: Opportunities to Promote Healthy Development and Well-Being for Children and Youth*, Washington, D.C.: National Academies Press, 2019a. As of November 17, 2020:
https://www.nationalacademies.org/our-work/summertime-experiences-and-child-and-adolescent-education-health-and-safety

National Academies of Sciences, Engineering, and Medicine, *Shaping Summertime Experiences: Opportunities to Promote Healthy Development and Well-Being for Children and Youth, Consensus Study Report Highlights*, Washington, D.C.: National Academies Press, 2019b. As of April 12, 2020:
https://www.nap.edu/resource/25546/Summertime%20Consensus.pdf

National Summer Learning Association, *Community Indicators of Effective Summer Learning Systems: Quick Reference Guide*, Baltimore, Md., June 2016. As of October 24, 2019:
http://www.summerlearning.org/wp-content/uploads/2016/06/NSLA-Community-Indicators-Quick-Reference-Guide_June-2016.pdf

NSLA—*See* National Summer Learning Association.

Office of the Deputy Mayor for Education, "About Learn 24," webpage, undated. As of November 11, 2020:
https://learn24.dc.gov/page/about-learn-24

———, "Bowser Administration Awards $4.8 Million in Summer Strong Grants," press release, Washington, D.C., April 12, 2019. As of November 11, 2020:
https://dme.dc.gov/release/bowser-administration-awards-48-million-summer-strong-grants

Schwartz, Heather L., Jennifer Sloan McCombs, Catherine H. Augustine, and Jennifer T. Leschitz, *Getting to Work on Summer Learning: Recommended Practices for Success*, 2nd ed., Santa Monica, Calif.: RAND Corporation, RR-366-1-WF, 2018. As of October 24, 2020:
https://www.rand.org/pubs/research_reports/RR366-1.html

StriveTogether, "Interactive Theory of Action: Emerging," webpage, 2019. As of October 24, 2019: https://www.strivetogether.org/interactive-theory-action/emerging/

U.S. Department of Education, "American Rescue Plan," webpage, undated. As of September 22, 2021: https://www.ed.gov/category/keyword/american-rescue-plan

Yoo, Paul Youngmin, Anamarie A. Whitaker, and Jennifer Sloan McCombs, *Putting Data to Work for Young People: A Ten-Step Guide for Expanded Learning Intermediaries*, Santa Monica, Calif.: RAND Corporation, TL-350-EHC, 2019. As of April 12, 2021: https://www.rand.org/pubs/tools/TL350.html